First Facts™

Holidays and Culture

Kwanzaa ~~WITHDRAWN~~

African American Celebration of Culture

by Amanda Doering

Consultant:
Sandra Adell, Professor of Literature
Department of Afro-American Studies
University of Wisconsin, Madison

Capstone
press

First Facts is published by Capstone Press,
151 Good Counsel Drive, P.O. Box 669, Mankato, Minnesota 56002.
www.capstonepress.com

Library of Congress Cataloging-in-Publication Data
Doering, Amanda.
    Kwanzaa: African American celebration of culture / by Amanda Doering.
    p. cm.— (First facts. Holidays and culture)
    Summary: "A brief description of the African American holiday of Kwanzaa, including how
it started and ways people celebrate this cultural holiday"—Provided by publisher.
    Includes bibliographical references and index.
    ISBN-13: 978-0-7368-5390-3 (hardcover)
    ISBN-10: 0-7368-5390-1 (hardcover)
    1. Kwanzaa—Juvenile literature. 2. African Americans—Social life and customs—Juvenile
literature. I. Title. II. Series.
GT4403.A2D64 2006
394.2612—dc22   2005020075

Editorial Credits
Christine Peterson, editor; Juliette Peters, designer; Robert Williams, illustrator; Wanda Winch,
    photo researcher; Scott Thoms, photo editor

Photo Credits
Capstone Press/Karon Dubke, 21
Corbis/Royalty-Free, cover, 1
Getty Images Inc., 16–17; Stephen Chernin, 20
The Image Works/Syracuse Newspapers, 9
PhotoEdit Inc/Kayte M. Deioma, 15; Patrick Olear, 18–19
SuperStock/Kwame Zikomo, 4–5
Unicorn Stock Photos/Aneal S. Vohra, 14; Robin Rudd, 6–7; Tommy Dodson, 13

1 2 3 4 5 6 11 10 09 08 07 06

Table of Contents

Celebrating Kwanzaa

A family gathers around a wooden candleholder. After lighting the black candle, family members share what **unity** means to them. They talk about African American leaders who united their **communities**. This family is celebrating the first day of Kwanzaa.

What Is Kwanzaa?

Kwanzaa is a holiday that celebrates African American history and **culture**. From December 26 to January 1, African Americans honor their **heritage** with food, music, and dancing. They remember the struggles of African people. Each night of Kwanzaa, people talk about ways to make their lives better.

How Kwanzaa Began

Kwanzaa was created by college professor Maulana Karenga in 1966. He wanted African Americans to remember their heritage and be proud of their culture.

Karenga based Kwanzaa on African **harvest** festivals. In Africa, people celebrate the harvest for seven days. Today, millions of African Americans continue this **tradition** during Kwanzaa.

Fact!

In the African language of Swahili, Kwanzaa means "first fruits."

Maulana Karenga, right, founder of Kwanzaa

9

Seven Principles of Kwanzaa

Umoja (oo-MOE-jah)

Unity

Joining together as families and communities

Kijuchagulia (koo-jee-cha-goo-LEE-ah)

Self-determination

Being responsible for yourself and your future

Ujima (oo-JEE-mah)

Collective work and responsibility

Working together to help each other and your community

Ujamaa (oo-JAH-mah)

Cooperative economics

Creating your own businesses and opportunities

Nia (nee-AH)

Purpose

Improving yourself, your family, and your community

Kuumba (koo-OOM-bah)

Creativity

Thinking of ways to make your life and community more beautiful

Imani (ee-MAH-nee)

Faith

Honoring African leaders, traditions, and culture

Seven Principles

Karenga based Kwanzaa on seven **principles** called the Nguzo Saba (n-GOO-zoh SAH-ba). These ideas are part of traditional African beliefs. Each night of the holiday, people talk about one principle. Families dance, tell African stories, or use songs to celebrate the day's principle.

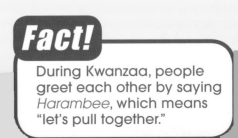

Fact!

During Kwanzaa, people greet each other by saying *Harambee*, which means "let's pull together."

Kwanzaa Symbols

Seven is an important number in Kwanzaa. Kwanzaa has seven principles and lasts seven days. The holiday also has seven **symbols**. Symbols represent the meaning of Kwanzaa. Together, Kwanzaa symbols and principles help people celebrate their African heritage.

Fact!

During Kwanzaa, families set out one ear of corn for each child.

Candles
Purpose—Seven Kwanzaa principles

Gifts
Creativity—Creativity
and giving

Unity cup
Cooperative economics
and Unity—
Family and community

Candleholder—African people

Crops
Collective work
and responsibility—
Traditional African
harvests

Corn
Self-determination—
Children and the future

Mat
Faith—African history
and traditions

13

Seven Candles

Kwanzaa candles symbolize the colors of Africa. The middle black candle stands for unity and the African people. It is lit on the first night.

Over the next six nights, children light
more candles. Three red candles stand
for the struggles of African people.
Three green candles represent hope.

16

Traditional Feast

On December 31st, families and communities join in the Kwanzaa feast of Karamu (kah-RAH-moo). Children sing and dance to the beat of drums. People bring traditional African or African American breads, fruits, and vegetables to share. During the feast, everyone drinks from a unity cup.

Kwanzaa Gifts

On the last night of Kwanzaa, children open gifts. Most Kwanzaa gifts don't come from stores. Instead, they are made by family members. Children receive books, African dolls, or beaded necklaces. Kwanzaa gifts help children learn more about their African heritage.

Amazing Holiday Story!

In New York City, African Americans gather during Kwanzaa to remember their ancestors. Each year, a Kwanzaa ceremony is held at the African Burial Grounds. At least 600 Africans were buried there. Many of them were slaves. During Kwanzaa, African American leaders honor the people buried there. Leaders pour water and say prayers to honor their ancestors.

Hands On: Make a *Mkeka*

A *mkeka*, or mat, holds the symbols of Kwanzaa during the seven-day celebration. Have an adult help you make a *mkeka*.

What You Need

scissors
red, green, and black
       construction paper
glue

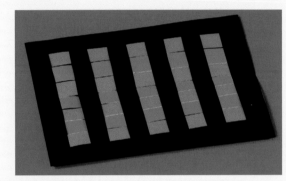

What You Do

1. Cut the red and green construction paper into long strips that are about 1 inch (2.5 centimeters) wide.
2. Fold the black paper in half lengthwise.
3. Cut into the fold, leaving 1 inch (2.5 centimeters) at the outer edge.
4. Continue to cut into the fold. Each cut should be about 1 inch (2.5 centimeters) apart. Unfold the black paper.
5. With a strip of red paper, begin weaving over and under across the black paper.
6. Weave a second row with a green strip of paper.
7. Continue weaving with red and green strips until the mat is complete.
8. Glue the loose edges when finished.

Glossary

community (kuh-MYOO-nuh-tee)—a group of people who live in the same area

culture (KUHL-chur)—a people's way of life, ideas, art, customs, and traditions

harvest (HAR-vist)—to collect and gather crops

heritage (HER-uh-tij)—history and traditions handed down from the past

principle (PRIN-suh-puhl)—a basic truth or belief; the seven principles of Kwanzaa can serve as guides for daily living.

symbol (SIM-buhl)—a design or an object that stands for something else

tradition (truh-DISH-uhn)—a custom, idea, or belief that is passed down through time

unity (YOO-ni-tee)—being together as one

Read More

Cooper, Jason. *Kwanzaa.* Holiday Celebrations. Vero Beach, Fla.: Rourke, 2003.

Gnojewski, Carol. *Kwanzaa: Seven Days of African-American Pride.* Finding Out About the Holidays. Berkeley Heights, N.J.: Enslow, 2004.

Internet Sites

FactHound offers a safe, fun way to find Internet sites related to this book. All of the sites on FactHound have been researched by our staff.

Here's how:
1. Visit *www.facthound.com*
2. Type in this special code **0736853901** for age-appropriate sites. Or enter a search word related to this book for a more general search.
3. Click on the **Fetch It** button.

FactHound will fetch the best sites for you!

Index